A Horse called H Bomb

By

Randy Stensaas

This is a work of fiction. Names, characters and incidents either are the products of the author's imagination or are used fictitiously, and any resemblance to actual persons, living or dead is entirely coincidental.

Copyright © 2010 RC Stensaas author

ISBN - 1453646981
ISBN-13 - 9781453646984

A Horse Called H Bomb

By

Randy Stensaas

## The beginning of the horse

There is not much to say about this ugly and I mean ugly horse.  He is a brown with white hair growing in where he had saddle sores he had them when we got him. His eyes are too wide, his ears not quit as big as a mules and his nose, wow, his nose, with that big Roman nose he could have smelled a gopher fart from ten miles away while underground.

We were at the horse sale in Billings in the spring, not really looking for anything but just drove up for the day and to watch. We had been there about an hour when they brought this old nag in.  I mean to tell you this thing was nag personified.  The poor cowboy riding him looked like heck, his shirt and pants were tore and he was riding like he was sitting on a cactus. He rode him around the ring a couple of times and I though the nag had handled fairly well. The guy swung down off of him and as he did he had an eye on the horse the whole time like the horse was going to bite him or blow up or something. I was surprised at that, that old nag didn't look like he had enough energy to fart, let alone buck. The guy pulled his saddle and bridle off and that horse and left the ring like he had a date.

That ugly old horse went over to the auctioneer booth and leaned up against it and believe it or not crossed his front legs. He was leaning over so far that if that booth had moved one inch he would have fell over.

The auctioneer looked at him and I have to give him credit he tried his best to get a bid out of that old nag but nobody was buying it, not even the dog food people, and when he leaned against the booth it got even worse, so I asked my dad to buy him, mainly because I felt sorry for him.  We picked up that sorry nag for $50 and I think that was an over payment, but I will give him credit after I got to riding him he would go all day and then some.

We loaded up and headed back down the road to home with our purchase in the back whinnying and sounding like he was singing a song.   After that he started pawing the floor of the truck like he was counting the miles go by, as if that wasn't enough he put the two together and actually made a decent tune out of it.

We made it home in one piece and was never so glad to see home as we were that day.  We could not have taken much more of the musical horse in the back.  We got him unloaded in the corral and figured we would see what we had the next day.

After a hearty meal of bacon, eggs, pancakes and a glass of milk I headed out to see what we had in the corral.  As I walked up and looked in I had to shake my head cause I couldn't believe I had told dad to buy such an ugly, emphasis on the word ugly, horse.

I crawled in to the corral and got a bridle out and walked up to him to bridle him up for the day. I put my arm around his neck and tried to slip the bridle on, he pulled his head back, I tried again, he put his head down, I tried again, he stuck his nose straight out, looking like a pointer. I tried one more time and this time he laid down and I couldn't move him or his head.

I thought you sorry buzzard I'll fix your sorry butt. So I walked over to the water tank and got a bucket full of water and came back. I asked him if he was going to get up and just laid there with his eyes closed ignoring me, so I poured that bucket of water in his ear. He jumped right up shaking his head. I grabbed him again and slipped the bridle right on.

"Now that wasn't so bad was it" I asked him.

He just looked at me, which was a trick in itself since his eyes were about as far apart as they could be without looking backwards. We walked over to the saddle shed and I threw the saddle on him, expecting problems, but no, he just stood that like he had been saddled a million times before. Which from looking at the white saddle scars on him he had.

I climbed on board and was prepared for him to start bucking at any moment but surprisingly we just trotted around the corral nice and easy like. He actually had a nice easy Tennessee walker kind of trot. I thought maybe this won't be so bad, may have actually ended up with a good work horse.

I started to say something to my mom, who was watching from the fence when all of a sudden I thought my head had been ripped off. That nag let out a big old fart, which I learned was his signature fart before he tried to kill you, and started bucking like he was a pro at it. We were all over that corral and I lasted about six jumps and hit the dirt on my back side. As soon as I left the saddle he stopped to watch me land and when I did he walked over and nuzzled me on the side of my face as if to say, 'come on you wimp, let's go again'.

I looked at him and being young and dumb, emphasis on dumb, I jumped up and got back on and slapped the spurs to him. He just humped up a bit and took off in the smoothest trot ever. I spurred him again and he moved up to an easy lope. I rode him around the corral for a while, and he would turn at the slightest touch of reins on his neck. In fact if I wasn't ready he would turn right out from under me. Hum might make a good cutting horse, must have been a good one in his day.

I rode over to the gate, reached down and opened it and took off out into the hay fields and pastures. I rode him around for about an hour and never had a bit of trouble with him, got my money's worth after all.

I rode over to a small pond to let him get a drink and he stuck his nose right in and took a big old slurp, and then it happened. He let out a big ol fart again and jumped right in the middle of that pond and went to bucking like he was the top bucking horse in the rodeo. The pond was only about one or two feet deep so it never slowed him up much.

I was pulling all the leather I could grab a hold of to keep from taking a bath, it didn't work, I splashed down flat on my back in that pond. I got my head back above water and when I looked around all I could see was the back end of that nag headed to the barn.

I crawled out and headed that way myself, fortunately it was only about a quarter of mile, but it was still early spring so it wasn't that warm yet. I got back to the barn and mom had the nag caught and was unsaddling him. She didn't seem too concerned that I wasn't on him, guess she figured I would walk home or they would find me the next day.

I walked up just as she got him turned loose and that sorry nag walked over to me, rubbed his nose against my face a couple of times as if to say sorry, see you tomorrow and took off. All I could do was just stand there and stare at him and call him names.

"You *&^%, you're not going to win, I will break you yet or you will be dog food" I yelled at him.

Mom and I walked back to the house where she cooked supper for us and dad asked how it went with the new horse. I told him about my day and what a worthless no good rotten snake in the grass that horse was. He asked other than that how was the day and the horse, I just said that horse and I were going to come to an agreement and it would be my agreement. It was going to be a long summer with the new horse.  But I had all summer and then some to make a horse out of that horse.

## A horse called H Bomb

This horse was winning; it has run away with me, bucked me off more times than I can count including at least once in a pond and let me walk home. Things had to change or he was going to win. To look at him standing around half asleep you would never know the evil that lurked.

Every time we had to work cows I had plenty of horses to choose from and I did, but I also couldn't let this old nag win so I would use him as often as I could.

We were out moving cattle around one day and things had gone fairly well with him, not one event, not one time did he try to kill me. Over all it was a good day, in fact I decided that I was winning. Wrong.

We were headed back home after a long, long, long day in the saddle, you know one of those days that starts before the sun is even a thought. Anyway we were finally finished and headed home when we came to the last hill before home, you could see home from the hill. It was not too steep and it was really just a big hill of loose dirt, good thing.

Any way I was relaxed, mistake, and had just kicked him over the edge and we were about ten feet down from the top when he let out a big fart. I don't know what it is about this horse and farts but he is very fond of letting one go, especially when he is getting ready to try and do me in. Anyway he let a big ol' fart that I know could have been heard in town and jumped straight up in the air and straight ahead about ten feet snapping my head back like it was on a hinge and came down with both front feet ramrod stiff in the dirt kicking his back legs straight up in the air. Me, when that happed I was history. I left that saddle like I had rockets in my pockets and landed face first in the dirt out in front of him and plowed the ground up for about five feet.

When I opened my eyes I was looking over a pile of dirt pushed up by my nose. When I got my eyes to focus I was also looking at funny looking rock I had plowed up with my face, an arrowhead. The only one I had every found in my young uneventful life. That still didn't excuse that brown nag.

My ears were ringing also, no wait, it was laughter. Max, my best friend and my mom were laughing themselves silly. My mom wasn't even concerned if I was ok, she was more concerned that I couldn't even ride an old nag of a horse; she carried on about what an embarrassment I was to the family, she was worse than Max.

I got up spitting out a mouth full of dirt a coughing and hacking like it was my last hour on earth. The way I felt with all that dirt in my mouth and up my nose I was thinking it might be better if it was my last hour.  I blew dirt out my nose for two days. That horse was going to pay.

I stood there looking at him and that was when I decided on the name for him; H Bomb.  It fit him because riding him was like sitting on a bomb you never knew when it was going to blow up or how big the explosion was going to be.   I told Max, my ever faithful partner in crime, and my mother the name and they looked at him for a minute and agreed that the name fit. He was stuck with it.

H Bomb was born.

I had been calling him names that you can't repeat in public for so long it took awhile to remember to call him that.

A few days later we had to go move cows again only this time they were across the Big Horn River that ran through our place.  It wasn't no small river either; it was probable 100 to 150 feet across.   It ran deep in lots of places but where we crossed it was about three feet as it ran over a rock base.

Anyway, you guessed it; I was on H Bomb again. Just something about that nag that kept drawing me back to him so I was on him for this gather. We all got to the river and everybody was crossing over but for some reason H Bomb kept refusing to cross. I finally got him going and we were headed across till we got right in the middle. There he stopped. He just refused to move another step no matter what I did. I kicked him, threatened to do him in, sell him for dog food it didn't matter he just stood there.

All of a sudden he just fell over like he was dead. He never gave me no warning, never farted which is always a tell tale sign with him; nothing, just fell over like he died of a heart attack, I should be so lucky, with me on him. I mean he never laid down like most horses do to roll in the water, he just fell over. It happened so fast I couldn't get out of the saddle. Right when he hit the water I managed to get my feet out of the stirrups but I was washed downstream about 100 feet before I could stop myself and get my feet under me.

Now it was a good thing it was warm or would have been long day. When I looked up at H Bomb he was on his feet again and standing on the shore looking at me like 'why you standing in the water stupid?' I sloshed out of the river and up to him figuring I was going to have to run his butt down but he just stood there waiting.

If I would have had a gun I would have made coyote bait out him right then, but I just climbed on board and shivering continued on my way. Took about an hour to dry out enough not to be shivering course Max had the gall to ask me why I fell out of the saddle crossing the river.

He said he was embarrassed to say he knew me if I couldn't ride any better than that. He went on and on like that for hours and I was about ready to let him have it when something amazing happened.

I think even H Bomb got tired of listening to Max ramble on cause we were standing resting for a minute when all of a sudden H Bomb turned with his butt toward Max, I tensed up cause I thought he was getting ready to fart and jump out from under me. He farted alright but it was just a little on the wet side and when I looked back there was Max sitting that nag he called a horse covered in horse crap. Guess all that green grass H Bomb had been eating finally worked its way through and it was all over Max.

Now as many times as he had tried to do me in I had to admit I was feeling pretty good about H Bomb at that moment cause now it was my turn to have a good laugh thanks to H Bomb, in fact I just about fell out of the saddle I was laughing so hard.

Max just sat there with a discussed look on his face trying to look dignified while covered in horse crap which just made it all the funnier to me. Kind of like the time Max was laughing at me when a red ant was biting the heck out of me and I was standing around with my pants down and my butt in the wind. I think we were close to even, but not quite.

We continued on our merry way moving cows, every time I would look at Max I would start laughing again. We were about finished and had to split up to make the last sweep, we said we would meet up at the house and took off our own directions.

I was riding along fat dumb and happy on H Bomb, a big mistake; guess I was still feeling good about him for what he did to Max. We were about two miles from home and I was riding along like I said, fat dumb and happy, half asleep, when H Bomb jumped sideways unseating me. I hit the ground with a thump looking around like, 'what happened?' I am a little slow at times.

When I looked up all I seen was the rear end of my horse with his tail straight up in the air and he was high tailing it for home as fast as he could go leaving me there with my butt on the ground and a long hike ahead of me. Twice in one day, this was getting too much even for somebody as slow as me.

I headed home and was cussing that horse every step of the way for about the first hundred steps. Then was cussing Max, just because it seemed the thing to do, because you know he would have been laughing himself silly at me again. I was cussing my boots because contrary to a popular song that was on the radio; these boots were not made for walking and by the time I got home my feet were hurting everywhere.

Of course the river was between me and home, so I was going to get wet again which did not improve my mood or my feet. Only good thing was I wasn't going to need a bath for a couple of weeks at least.

When I walked in to the yard H Bomb was standing by the saddle shed just waiting for me like nothing happened. Max showed up about the same time I did, which didn't help cause he could see I was wet again from the river and could see H Bomb standing about 100 feet from where I was.

Being highly intelligent like he is he put two and two together, got three, and started laughing. I was just too pooped to care. I walked over and led H Bomb to the shed took the saddle off, whispered in his ear that there would be another day and to watch out at which point he just blew his nose in my face and took off at a high run for the pasture.

One of these days…………………one of these days………………POW.

## Do I want to be a cowboy with a horse like H-bomb

I can't believe I wanted to be a cowboy. It was summer again. I was helping on the ranch breaking horses and getting cows ready to move to another pasture. Of course to do this you had to get up early, real early, like five o'clock early. This is for the birds. Now, I want you to know that I am not a morning person. I don't even try to talk to anybody till I've brushed my teeth and had a drink of water, in that order. So I am not much of a socialite for an hour or more and today was no different. Mom had breakfast ready and is always talkative.

I walked into the kitchen, "Morning. You how you want your eggs" mom asked.

Me; "Grunt", got a drink "Over easy".  I am just a fountain of words first thing in the morning.

This morning we were going to move cows off the BLM and get them ready to go to summer pasture on the mountain. Mom and Dad were going to go one way and work a pasture and I was going the other way and work a different pasture.

Like I said part of my job is to break horses.  Now this sounds easy but it is a job where you get all the chances to kill yourself that you want.  In fact somebody once said, "A horse breaker is a cowboy with his brains kicked out."  I tend to agree with him.

Anyway this morning we went to the corral to catch our horses for the day.  I had planned to take a big brown hammer-headed horse called H-bomb that we had bought at the horse sale in Billings a while back.  This horse was something else and had bucked me off in a pond, in the middle of nowhere and left me afoot numerous times.  To say that he was coming along fairly well, would be an over statement of the facts of life.  But I had to ride him, he was winning.

I got my rope on him and tried to get him tied up to saddle.  This happened only after we made about three trips around the corral, with my boot heels plowing up the ground.  Then somehow, I got ahead of my feet and was flipped loose from the end of the rope and came to a sudden stop against the corral with my feet against the top rail and my head against the bottom rail.  As I slid down the fence to the ground, I thought to myself "I got out of bed for this abuse?"

Eventually I got H-bomb tied up and started to brush him down and kind of careless like I bent over and walked under his neck to the other side.

Good Lord Almighty a mountain lion ran in the corral and bit me right on the butt. I spun around cussing and hollering and there stood that brown skunk looking like he was asleep, with a piece of my pants in his month.

Mom hollered over at me, "what's the matter? Get stepped on?"

"Heck no" I said, "This dirty rotten skunk just bit me in the butt."

Well that made me so mad, I grabbed the saddle off the ground, threw it on him and cinched her down as tight as I could, then I kneed him in the stomach to knock the air out of him and cinched her down some more.

I then went and changed my pants. When I came back out he was standing there still looking like he was more asleep then awake. I got on him kind of easy like not sure what to expect but not wanting to ruin another pair of pants. I had had enough of him already and the day had not started yet.

Most of the day went along pretty well. That old brown only ran through the brush with me twice and when that didn't get rid of me he seemed to give up for the day. Around five o'clock I was making one last pass through the pasture to be sure we had not missed any cows.

Careless like I kicked him in to an easy lope and relaxed to enjoy the ride, the wind was blowing easy like around me and the day was finishing up pretty good. I mean the sun was shining, the birds were singing and old brown was behaving himself life was good.

Then I pulled on the reins to slow him up and felt my pleasant moment vanish, life was not good any more. The chin strap broke, it was all downhill from there if you can imagine. When that brown horse felt the strap break he was gone. I mean to say we were off to the races. The wind wasn't blowing easy like anymore it was more like a hurricane now. I couldn't feel the sun shining on me anymore we out ran it and the birds had quit singing, heck they were sucked up in the vortex behind us.

In an effort to stop this wreck waiting to happen I was pulling on those reins like I was pulling a pot of gold out of a deep well. All to no avail, no matter what I did nothing was stopping that run away brown. I was cussing that brown horse every jump of the way. I cussed the bridle for breaking. I cussed myself for being so stupid as to not check the bridle to make sure it was ok.

We came down off a long hill just a flying, I mean to tell you we put those nags that run in the Kentucky Derby to shame. No matter what I did I could not get that brown to stop or even slow up.

My eyes were watering so bad from the wind that I couldn't see anything, not that there was anything to look at anyway. Then I realized that the way he was going he was going to run right pass an old corner post that had been part of a fence line that had disappeared who knows when. Only this one old post was left. I was thinking to myself "I'll stop you now you SOB."

I took down my rope and tied it off hard and fast to the horn, shook out a loop and waited till we streaked by that post. As we went past that post I dropped the loop over it.

Now who would have imagined that an old fence post would turn to concrete and grow roots that reached halfway to China?

When I came to sometime later, not sure how much later but later; I looked around on a very strange sight. As I looked back the way we had come from I could see that fence post off in the distance with my rope still around it. At the end of the rope was a saddle, looked like my saddle but it was not looking too good. About twenty feet from the saddle toward me laid that old brown horse, looking like he was dead. I should be so lucky. From H-bomb there was a furrow in the ground that ended right where I was sitting.

I got unsteadily to my feet and limped over to where H-bomb was. As I was looking at him, he blinked; he wasn't dead, too bad. It took awhile and some work to get him back on his feet. He didn't look any steadier on his feet than I felt, we made a pair. I walked him over to where my saddle lay, there was no use putting it on him it was in no shape to use. I would have to come back for it later.

I fixed the bridle with a strap off my spurs, and then I looked at H-bomb and then looked in the direction of home. I thought about walking, then I thought about how far it was, looked at my boots which were not made for walking so I looked at H-bomb again. I thought "what the heck" and swung up on him bareback and headed home.

He had a backbone like a saw blade and it was not doing my sore butt any good. With my sore rear end getting sorer with every step on his bony backbone, I was thinking death couldn't come soon enough.

It was late when we got back to the ranch, but at least H-bomb had behaved his self all the way home. He was a little wobbly on the way home; I think he was as shook up from that sudden stop as I was. I turned him loose in the corral and hung the bridle on a post. The sight of that post made me shudder.

I limped into the house and sat down at the table. "How did it go today?" mom asked.

I hurt all over and all I wanted to do was sleep for a week, so I just said "you know how it is, just another day trying to break that old brown horse, to no avail."

I couldn't wait for Max and me to get together again. This being a cowboy and trying to break that old brown nag that passed for a horse was for the birds.

## The Horse The ant and Me

Well, I know I shouldn't but we had to gather cattle to move and I figured it had been awhile since I had ridden H-bomb, the ol Brown nag, so I caught him and got saddled up. I had named him H Bomb, because you never knew when he was going to blow up and try to do you in again. But we had to ride and he was around, besides it was time for him to get a work out again. He had been pretty good since the wreck we had when he run away with me and I dropped the rope over the post. Boy did we come to a stop. It took a few days before H Bomb was his normal self but he recovered and not only that he recovered faster than I did.

We rode for a few hours before we got to where the cows were after we got there we started to work them getting them rounded up to move. Things were going fairly well and H Bomb was behaving himself, unbelievable.

In fact he was doing so good I had taken down my rope and Max and I were heeling the calves and letting them go. Things were starting to look up with this horse and thinking he might turn into a good rope horse yet. I shook out another loop was swinging it and just as I was about to throw he let out a big windy and jumped sideways. I took a grab at the saddle horn to keep from being unseated but it was not there. I then looked down and there was no horse under me anymore either. This did not bode well as I was in the middle of about a million acres of cactus.

I hit the ground on my butt with my eyes closed because I knew I was sitting in a cactus pile. But I didn't feel anything so I slowly opened my eyes and looked around. I had landed in the only place in thirty square feet without any cactus however it did have an ant hill worse yet a red ant hill and I was sitting right on top of it. But they were not out in force yet, that is until I landed on their home. Just as I looked down they started to swarm out in the millions.

I jumped up and started stomping and jumping around to get them off. The brown buzzard I was riding was only a couple of feet away, just standing there looking at me, like I was the village idiot. I ran over there and grabbed the reins climbed on board and moved off before them ants ate us.

I checked myself over and didn't see any of the little red buggers, so life was good again. I looked over at Max and he was having a laughing fit. I mean it was terrible the way he was carrying on, he could barely stay in the saddle he was laughing so hard that talking to him was out of the question with him.

I just looked at him, "You know you could have helped a little, at least show some concern that I might be hurt." He just looked at me and started laughing again; Disgusting.

We moved on heading out to finish what we had started. We had been riding along slow and easy for about twenty minutes moving the cows ahead of us.

"Yowwwwwwwwww" I yelled as I jumped off H Bomb and was dancing around like I was having a fit. Max's horse had jumped sideways at my outburst about unseating him and of course the cows took off in 360 different directions. Max was looking at me like I had gone mad. "What's wrong with you now?"

I never answered; I was too busy jerking my pants down. After I got them down with my bare butt in the wind there was a red ant biting things that were best left unbitten. I was jumping around so bad it took a couple of tries to grab the little bugger, but I finally managed get him off and the relief was mind boggling. I just stood there with the wind blowing around my bare behind and other parts and sighed with relief, there is no way to really describe how wonderful it felt.

I looked over at Max and he was lying on the ground beside his horse laughing so hard he was holding his sides; every time he would stop laughing a little he would look over at me with my pants down around my ankles and my butt in the wind and would go into another fit of laughter. It was getting embarrassing the way he was caring on.

With as much dignity as I could muster I pulled my pants back up and climbed back on board H Bomb. I swear that horse was even grinning at me.

I sat there waiting for Max to get back on his horse so we could continue. He finally managed to get back on and we headed off again, however every time he would look at me he would bust out again.

I don't know how he stayed on his horse, good thing he was riding a nag.

Like I said when I let out that blood curdling yell the cows had scattered every which way like their tails were on fire, which meant that we had to go find them all again and start over. Course Max did not let me forget that either, he kept reminding me that if not for me we would be back at home now. Yea sure blame the poor boy that was getting ate by the ant, like it was all his fault.

The way Max was carrying on I could see that this little adventure was not going to go away for me anytime soon even though I was just as happy to forget it. I am sure when he told the story later it would not even be close to the real story. There was nothing I could do about it, but my day would come, somehow, somewhere, it would be my turn to laugh myself silly at him, oh yeah it would come, ever ant has his day.

## H Bomb on the road again

Every year we would have to drive our cattle to the mountains where they would spend the summer eating and getting fat. This was done by a good old fashion trail drive, yea the kind you read about in the westerns. We would spent a week gathering the cows off the BLM pastures around the ranches and get them bunched to head to the mountains.

Course this takes horses, yes this was long before the 4 wheelers, a four wheeler in my day was a four wheel drive pickup. It was a long, long time ago in a state far, far, away from the now world. It was before anything now.

It was so far away that I remember when we got the first phone we were all so excited that everybody just stood around the phone waiting for it to ring, at least Max and I did. It was a wall mount phone and if you picked it up you could hear people talking; miracle. We had a party line so everybody in the country was on the same line and knew everybody's business. Amazing what you could learn if you picked up the phone in the old days; enough rambling back to the cattle drive.

Of course if there are horses involved you got it, H Bomb was there. This horse was winning again and I had to get ahead of the game or I was going to be sidelined. So I rounded him up and got ready for the drive. He just stood there like the well broke horse he wasn't. I knew it was all a ruse; he was just waiting for the right moment, like now.

I was currying him down to saddle, yea can you believe it I was being nice to him. Anyway I was currying him down and had a brain fart and forgot what I was doing, but not for long.

The *^%@* had moved and was standing on my foot. I was trapped; there was 900 pounds of H Bomb standing on my toes. Well almost, thankfully my boots were just a little big and he was on the end, I couldn't wiggle my toes either that was for sure, but I was fairly trapped. All I could do was jump around on one foot, call him names and beat on him; it didn't matter; I was trapped like a bug in a rug.

I couldn't get the boot off cause it was too tight with him standing on it. All I could do was stand and wait until he decided it was time to move. He looked around at me and grinned, yes grinned, what can I say, one of us is mental and I think it's the horse. After the exchange of grins he moved off my foot. I slapped a saddle on him before anything else happened and took off.

We were out getting things moving and cattle into a herd to take to the mountains in a couple of days. After the foot standing incident he was behaving himself again, something was up.

We had found a bunch of cows and were moving them along nice and easy. H-Bomb and myself were following along nice and easy like. H Bomb had his head down swinging it back and forth grabbing a bunch of grass every third or fourth sweep. I would pull it back up and after a few minutes he would have it back down swinging back and forth again. His head was moving back and forth so much it was a wonder it didn't snap off.

Also of a sudden a calf took off. H Bomb jerked his head up jumped out after him before I had time to think about it. I was thinking this was a cow horse, feeling kind of proud of him. What can I say? I'm a slow learner.

We were headed toward a fence and that calf just jumped right through it, huh oh, I thought; H Bomb is going to jump it too. I got ready for H Bomb to jump the fence when at the last second he cut back to the right. Me on the other hand never, I just kept going straight right into the fence. At the last second I got turned around in mid air so I hit the fence with my back. I stretched that fence about five feet and when it got to the end it snapped back and shot me out of there like I was in a sling shot. I went flying back though the air like a big assed bird. My arms and legs were flapping and clawing trying to get anything they could to stay airborne. It wasn't the flight that was the problem it was going to be the landing I was not looking forward to.

Like I said my arms and legs were flapping like a cat doing an impression of a bird, everything was moving but nothing was working. I did manage to look up just as the fence launched me, to see Max show up. Of course his jaw was open about a foot cause when he saw me I was headed right toward him. Not good.

He tried to move but I landed on him and we both fell to the ground. My landing was not too bad, Max was under me. Of course when I flew into him he was on his horse which of course I knocked him off of. When we landed his horse took off at high speed to the barn, H Bomb was already gone. That left us to; yep you guessed it, walk.

I was getting more time on my feet with that horse then I was getting on my butt in the saddle. However this time I was not walking alone and for some reason Max didn't see the humor in it. Can't understand it, he always found the humor in when it was me, strange.

## H-bomb and the rodeo

When I was in high school along with Max, yea we both made it to high school I know you're surprised; you had to be in the high school rodeo club. Of course we were, and guess what, we rode bulls, I know you're surprised about that.

Of course I had H Bomb to rope on so I was doing some calf roping also. This old fart had turned into a fairly decent roping horse. I know, I couldn't believe it myself but I had been roping off of him every time I rode him. This was all the time cause I couldn't let him win and I was trying to wear him down. It wasn't working, he was wearing me out, but couldn't let him get wind of that.

We were at the local rodeo and the day was actually going good. We were in the first day of a two day rodeo and I was in the calf roping first and then the bull riding later. Max was just in the bull riding events along with me which would be the last event of the day.

H-bomb and I got called up so we entered the roping pen and I backed his big butt into the corner. His little pig eyes was looking all over the place and I leaned over and whispered in his ear, "You screw up here buster and when we get home you're going to be coyote bait. You understand me?" He just wiggled an ear at me.

I settled back in saddle, got my rope tucked under my arm and looked at the calf chute and back down, kind of nodding to get my neck loose. The guy running the gate thought I nodded for the calf and opened the gate. I was not set when the gate flew open and the calf was gone and so were we, or I should say H-bomb was gone. When that gate opened he let a big ol fart and jumped about 30 feet out in the arena. However I was not there with him. When he made that jump my head snapped back and I did a back flip right off his butt landing face down in the dirt.

When I looked up, and I didn't want to, he was out in the arena looking back at me like 'what you doing back there? The calf is out here.' Of course the whole place was roaring in laughter, besides the clowns I was funniest thing going on. I got up, took a bow to save a little dignity, and then I walked over to that nag and made a pistol out of my hand using my finger and thumb, pointed it at him and said "bang". That smart ass horse fell over like he was dead, getting even more laughs out of the crowd.

It was so bad the clowns came over and wanted to know if the horse and I wanted to join them for the summer rodeo season. They said that we were the funniest show they had seen and that we had gotten more laughs than they had. I told them no, that this nag was going to the dog food factory when I left here.

I grabbed his reins and got him back up, crawled on board and slunk out of there, glad that was over.

I met up with Max and told him I was going to haul H-bomb to the dog food factory when we left. He just nodded his head and agreed. We sat around for the next few hours till the bull riding started and then we were back into the thick of things again. The one good thing about this rodeo was that Max's dad was the stock contractor so we knew about the bulls, but that didn't help we still had to draw them just like everybody else.

We got to the chutes and Max got on a big ol Black Angus bull. I helped him get settled and got the rope pulled up tight and the next thing Max was nodding and the gate was open and away he went. It was a great ride, for about two seconds. That bull jumped left, Max went with him, then in mid air the bull went right and Max was still going left. One two three and it was over, I could see we needed more time on that bucking barrel.

I got on my bull which happened to be a small Brahma, and I was remembering all the barrel rides, the mutton busting rides and calf rides and boy was I ready. They opened the gate and away I went, he jumped out there bucking and kicking and I actually thought I was doing good; in my dreams.

I opened one eye; the world was spinning out of control so I shut it. I opened the other eye it was a little better so I managed to open both eyes. I was surprised not to see dirt, instead I seen white walls and white bedding, I don't remember the arena having anything white, I must be in heaven. I looked around some more and figured out I wasn't in heaven but in the hospital. Now as strange as that seemed to me what was even stranger, was I was hungry.

Now that was not the weird part, the weird part was the fact that I was hungry for liver and onions. You have to realize I never liked them before, yuck. But now all of a sudden I was craving liver and onions, too weird.

My parents came to the hospital, paid my ransom and got me out and I told them I was wanting liver and onions. Mom looked at me like I had hit my head, surprise I did, or so they told me. I guess that I went off over the front of that bull and he decided to see if my head was harder than his, it wasn't.

Then after I was on the ground he decided to use me for a door mat and walked the length of me a couple of times, he then stopped looked at me, licked my face a couple of times to make sure I was ok, like he was sorry, before he decided to go back to his pen and rest up. Anyway that is the story Max told me later.

And here all this time I thought H-bomb was trying to kill me, I may have to give him a second change since he was a sissy compared to that bull ride. Maybe the dog food factory would have to wait. There was always another day for that.

# H Bomb and the Campout

Up in the northwest corner of Wyoming is Cody, home of Buffalo Bill Cody among other things. West of there was the Rocky mountains, along with Yellowstone park. But not everything was Yellowstone; there is the Absoraka wilderness area.

We had a friend who every summer he would go down the south fork out of Cody and about eight miles into the wilderness area in a canyon there used to be an old mining camp. He was retained by the mining company to go in there every year and do work so they could keep their mining claims.

This year he took Max and me along for the ride and the camping. So we loaded up and hauled the horses to the end of the

South Fork and unloaded and headed out. Of course we had to ford the South Fork River, which made me a little apprehensive since I was riding H-bomb and he liked to lay down it the water. But we made it across and headed out.

It was about eight miles back to the mining camp and even for an old county boy like me I have to admit that the country was beautiful. We followed a trail cut into the side of the mountain with the river about a thousand feet below. After about 3 hours of riding the trail opened it to a great little valley and we could see the cabins below.

We rode down and the horses that the old fart had were house pets so he turned them loose behind the cabins in a box canyon till he was ready to leave. I on the other hand was riding H-bomb who would love nothing more than running home without me and lazing around the barn all day. So Max and I put out horses in a corral that was there. We checked it and it looked good and solid.   We then proceeded to get set up for the weekend.

Bud, the old fart, had a big hunting tent and he set it up outside the cabin on a wood floor that was there.  I thought what the heck, here is a nice log cabin with stove and chairs and beds in it and we are in a tent, but it was his show.

We got all settled in and he proceeded to cook supper for us and we just sit around and yakked the night away or till about ten o'clock.   We all crawled in our sleeping bags and when to sleep.  Along about two in the morning, according to my watch, I heard something outside the tent grunting and snorting; bear.

Now remember I still was not over the movie, 'Night of the Grizzly' where a big mean ol' grizzly bear was killing cows and stuff on a ranch, not far from where we were now camped in fact.   This is not boding well for me.  I know that bear is outside my bedroom window every night waiting for me, now he has found me sleeping in a tent. A tent of all things, I'm dead.

"Max you hear that"?

"Yea" he replied, "it must be just outside waiting for us to go to sleep."

"Would you two shut up, you're going to bore it to death with all your talking" came the reply from Bud, "good grief".

I crawled down into my sleeping bag with just my eyes and ears showing and tried to sleep, but no matter how hard I tried to stay awake, I fell asleep anyway.

We hung out for a couple of days fishing and wandering around while Bud worked in the mine doing his thing. We checked on our horses to make sure they were alright and had food. Every time we would look in on them H-bomb would be looking back at me, like this is heaven can we stay forever. I thought maybe he is working out yet.

The last day finally came and we got up and ate breakfast and I went to check on the horse to get them ready to leave and when I got there the pen was empty. I stood there looking at it like my eyes were lying to me. I blinked a couple of times and looked about and finally seen where they had knocked down a couple of logs from the fence and were gone.

I let out a string of cuss words and ran around to where the fence was down and looked at the tracks and they were leaving out of there on a run. I followed along for about a mile and they were headed down the road to home, without me. Dirty rotten no good, SOB, and every other thing I could think of to call him. I just stood looking down the tail for a few minutes and walked back to the camp and told Max and Bud the good news.

Bud said he would put our saddles on the pack horses but we would have to walk out to the truck. He said we couldn't ride because he wasn't coming back for the stuff after he left. Yea right, he was in cahoots with H-bomb and was just making us walk.

So off we headed back out the way we came. It was nice long hike and took us most of the day to do it. The hike wasn't the problem it was the river we had to wade across when we got back to the trucks. Once we got there, there was no way around it, we had to wade across. Fortunately it was only about 3 feet deep and 100 feet across. But it was still a pain cause of the big rocks in it. If you fell you got washed downstream about half mile before you could get stopped so it was best not to fall down.

We managed to get across and were sitting in the sun drying when Bud came riding up. Thankfully it was mid August and the weather was nice and warm otherwise we would have been a couple of popsicles sitting there.

We loaded up and headed home and I didn't care at that point where that stupid horse was at. If I never seen him again it would be too soon. Well too soon showed up, it was about two weeks later when I went out to the corral one morning and there he stood, looking at me like nothing had happened. I took one look at him and just shook my head, 'no you are not going to get to me' I thought. Dog food would be too good for you, cat food would be too good for you and bad for the cats, I'm thinking maybe turning you in to a plow horse and make you drag a plow around all day may be the answer. Yep that definitely has a sound to it; I may have to look in to it.

## H-bomb and trick riding

I grew up in a family that all grew up on ranches working cows and horses. My mother grew up in western South Dakota during the depression and WWII and on into the fifties and on. Riding was a way of life and during this time she broke a bunch of Shetland ponies to ride. She told me later that they were a pain to break, worse than full size horses.

During this time the movies were also the big entertainment of the time, western movies especially. My mom did all the trick riding stuff that you would see them doing in the movies back then. She would take off on a lope with the horse and drop down on one side and hit the ground with both feet the momentum bouncing her across to the other side where it was repeated until she decided to land in the saddle. She would also do what can best be described as handstands on the horse while it loped in a circle. To do this she would lean across the saddle till face down on one side and holding on to the saddle horn and straps on the back of the saddle and then put her feet straight up in the air, doing an effective handstand, as the horse would lope around the corral. I watched her do all this stuff in the old home movies we had. You remember the old 8mm movies of the day? This was eons before video and digital videos.

Well of course after hearing these stories about trick riding and seeing mom do them on the movies I had to try it. I talked to my best friend Max about it and he thought it was a great idea also. So with the thought planted and getting watered everyday it was growing it was only a matter of time till we had to try it.

The day came and we got our horse out to do our tricks on, well guess what the only one that was available for me was H-bomb. I looked at him dismayed; I just knew he was going to try and kill me. But if we were going to do this we had to use him. We got smart, a first I know, and never left the corral. We figured that way there was less room for them to run away.

Max went first on his nag he got her loping around the corral at a nice slow pace and he got both feet on one side and his head on the other and miracles of miracles he did a head stand hanging on the side of the horse. I just stood there dumb founded I couldn't believe it. He even managed to get back down and in the saddle. Miracles never cease.

Well it was my turn so I kicked H-bomb in to a lope and we go round and round and round. Max yelled if I was going to do it or not, or was I chicken. Well I knew I had to do it or I would never live it down so I get laid across the saddle and I grab the horn and the straps and I manage to get my legs in the air. I was doing it, I was doing it, huh oh, huh oh, I could feel my legs going on over. I tried to stop them and get them back up but it was to no avail. I went on over and off landing on the ground on my back with a thump.

"Am I dead" I managed to squeak out.

"Nah, you're fine, now get up and quit lying around" was the response I got out of Max; lots of sympathy there.

I got back up and of course there stood H-bomb just looking at me like he was a sleep. I walked over and got back on and away we went again. I tried it again and guess what, I had the same results.

"Am I now dead" I asked.

"Nope, you're not very good at that are you?" Max said.

Well I got back up and there stood H-bomb, surprise. The one time I wanted him to run away and there he stood, dang. I got back on but I wasn't going to try that again so this time I decided to do the bouncing thing.

I got him going again and I got down on his left side hanging on the saddle with my feet about a foot off the ground as we went around the corral, I swallowed and dropped my feet down and before I knew it I was back up and sitting in the saddle. It worked; holy crap it worked. Yahoo I yelled and ripped my hat off and threw it in the air.

I thought this worked so good I stopped and got my hat and we did it again, this time I bounced all the way to the other side and then back to the saddle. This is great, something I could actually do and H-bomb was actually behaving.

Max and I congratulated each other on what we accomplished. I could do the bouncy thing and he could do the head stand thing. So every time we when riding for the next few weeks we kept practicing and we actually got good at it.

Another rodeo was coming up, remember in Wyoming in the summer there are rodeos every weekend somewhere. So we were entered in the next rodeo and when the weekend came around we headed out.

Of course I was going to try calf roping again and on H-bomb, besides the bull riding. Every since the first rodeo when I got walked all over by a bull and H-bomb jumped out from under me in the calf roping I have been working his butt off and he was better at it now. How dumb can I get?

Anyway we are at the rodeo and the first day went fairly well, I actually managed to catch the little bugger and get a time, I know my grandmother could have done it faster, but hey I caught the little bugger and got a time, I was happy.

The next day we were at it again and my turn came up for the roping. I get H-bombs big butt backed into the chute, get the rope tucked, looked at the calf and this time I did nod and we were off. H-bomb caught that calf in about three jumps, a lot faster than I could get my rope in action but after a second of hesitation I got that rope out and around the little buggers' neck. H-bomb slammed on the brakes and I jumped off and threw the calf to the ground made three fast loops around his feet and jumped back with my arms in the air, TIME.

I was dumbfounded I had actually did it and as I sat there listening I heard the announcer tell the crowd I had done it in 16 seconds. I was ecstatic I was actually in the money.

I felt so good I decided to show off and show them the trick riding I had learned. I turned H-bomb around and loped back and as I was doing this I got down on his left side and I did the bouncy thing to the other side and back. The crowd loved it so I decided to do it one more time and I got down hit the ground and when I was going over H-bombs back with my legs struck straight out behind me he slammed on the brakes.

I shot over his head like I had been shot out of cannon landing about ten feet out in front of him. I didn't want to move I could hear the crowd laughing and having a great time then I felt something beside me. I looked over and there stood H-bomb looking at me and then the smartass put a hoof on my back, not heavy, but he put it there pinning me to the ground like bug on a board and then he whinnied as loud as he could a couple of times and the crowd went nuts with laughter.

I crawled out from under his foot and stood up and here came the clowns again. They ran up and made a big scene of bushing me off and going over to H-bomb and pretending to try and lift him up on their shoulders, the crowd was eating it up.

They asked me again to join them because I had to be working out this act with the horse because there was no way that this was not planned. I just looked at them and told them not yet, this horse may be cat food before too long. With that said

I gathered up the reins and climbed on and rode out the best round of applause that day.

The day was over and we loaded up and headed back home, Max had placed in the bull riding so he had some money, I had placed in the calf roping and had some money so we were happy but I was beginning to wonder about that horse. Every rodeo so far he been the hit of the crowd, I may have to re-think the clown offer, I might get a good price for him, it is a thought.

## Shoeing H-bomb

Of course living on a ranch we had horses and these were working horses. Working horses meant we had to shoe them. So I had been messing with horses since I was old enough to walk and riding before that, yea my mom would put a pillow in front of her on the saddle sit me on it and we would head off to visit the neighbors back in the old days of yore.

So anyway I had been cleaning hooves for what seemed like forever. I learned and got started on a pony we had, he was about three forth's the size of a horse and was called Champion, after Gene Autry's horse. Anyway I would pick up his feet and hold it and clean away. He was good about it and liked to have his feet worked on. He would just stand there and let you work away. He would look back at you every so often to see if you were ok or at least that was what I thought he was doing.

He was the same horse I learned to shoe on also. The prefect horse to learn on and for kids to ride, and even then he was tough as nails. I would jump on him and take off riding on the cows for a couple hours or more ever so often and he was as fresh when we got back as when we left.

H-bomb was a horse of a different sort when it came to shoeing; believe it or not he liked it. Yea I couldn't believe it either, but it didn't take long to figure out why.

It was time for a shoeing and I walked out to the corral and looked in and just about turned around and went back to the house for some more coffee. H-bomb was the only one in there and the only one left, all the rest were done. I looked at him and he looked at me, each of us sizing the other one up. I kept looking at him and I wasn't sure that he wasn't dead on his feet I was just about ready to go push on him and see if he fell over but he finally blinked.

I sighed and entered the corral and got him caught and ready to shoe. He was just as charming as he could be; he did everything I needed him to do so I could shoe him. I got all my stuff out and ready and picked up his front foot and went to cleaning away. Amazingly I managed to do all his feet and he just stood there watching me. I finished and looked at him like I couldn't believe it, this can't be H-bomb.

I walked up and talked to him a minute bragging him up and scratching behind his ears, which he loved and got ready to finish up. I should have known something was up with him.

I picked up a front foot and got all situated to file and put the shoe on. Man it must be time for lunch or something; I can't believe how heavy I feel, feeling weak in fact.    I braced my legs and hunched my shoulders and continued for a minute. Good grief what is going on, I feel like I am holding the weight of the world on my shoulders. Then it hit me, I looked over my shoulder and that rotten SOB was leaning, more like laying, on me like I was a leaning post.    In other words I was holding this heavy buzzard up.    I dropped his foot and jumped sideways out of the way and he was leaning so heavy on me and about half asleep that when I moved he actually fell down.

"That will teach you, you sorry excuse for a horse" I told him, "now get your butt back up and knock it off" as I grabbed the rope and got him back up.

I got him ready to go again and finished up the hoof and moved to the back one. At least with the back feet it is harder for him to do anything because of the way the leg is held.    So the back two feet actually went fairly fast now on to the last one.

I picked up the front foot again and went to work; I was sweating away when he started feeling heavy again. I dropped that foot and jumped out of the way but he never fell over this time, I think I moved before he got totally relaxed. I walked over and slapped him in the belly and told him to knock it off. I picked up the foot again, same story. After what seemed like an hour on just that one foot I finally got him finished. The sweat was just a streaming off of me at that point.

I leaned against him for a minute and slipped the halter off of him and started to walk to the saddle shed. I had just taken about two steps when I felt him grab me by the back of my pants by my belt. I tried to turn around and I couldn't and the next thing I know he had me picked up in his month , no matter how much I wiggled or squirmed I couldn't get free, I was like worm on a hook.

In those days I was a skinny kid, now days he would have to use a crane, so he picked me up and took off walking. I was trying to see where he was going when I seen the water tank coming up. No, this can't be happening, but it was. He walked up to it and dropped me right in, SPLASH.

I thought you sorry son of a gun, dirty rotten no good buzzard, you are history. But he just stood there looking at me like, 'there you feel better?' I had to admit it was hot and I was hot and the water did cool me off and felt good, after I got over the shock.

My mom walked out to see if I was finished and got to the corral just about the time that H-bomb picked me up and headed to drop me in the tank. When I looked over at her she was having a good laugh.

"You should have seen yourself" she said, "You looked just like a worm on a hook wiggling around."

The more I thought about it the funnier it got and I had to admit H-bomb had done me a good deed by cooling me off, but I couldn't let him know that. He was winning more than I was and that was not in the game plan. I crawled out of the tank, patted him on the side of the neck and said "next time it is my turn."

He looked at me shook his head a couple of times and turned around and high tailed it out to the pasture through the gate that mom had opened. I just shook my head, I was actually starting to like that cuss.

## The Trail Drive
## H Bomb and me again

Well it took awhile but we were finally ready to head to the hills, no really, we were driving the cattle to the mountains for the summer where they would spend all summer eating and getting fat. Max and I and everybody else has been working for the last couple of weeks getting the cattle rounded up off of the BLM for the drive.

Course I had to ride that no good horse H Bomb part of the time on the gather. I had to, couldn't let him think he was winning but the current score was H-bomb 10, me zero. Not a good score so with that in mind I had to stay in the game and try to even it up a little. As you can imagine I rounded him up for the drive.

The drive started at the ranches and proceeded to the mountains about 15 miles to the east of us. It would take a day to get to the foot of the mountains and then a day and they would be on the top. That should be enough time to put the score in my favor with H Bomb.

We were under way, leaving at the crack of dawn, not my favorite time of day. In those days all the ranches had cow dogs, these things were life savers as they would work the brush where you couldn't get on horseback and the cows love to run in there and hide. So the dogs would go in barking and biting, you would hear the brush moving and cows running and before you knew it out would pop a cow with a dog hanging on its tail or nipping its heels.

There was an old cow that ran in the brush in front of me and no matter how much yelling I did she won't move. I looked all around and there were no dogs around to help either. So I looked at H Bomb, looked at the brush and thought ok, so I headed him into the brush. He swiveled his ears back at me like I lost my mind, but then he looked forward and I could see him thinking "I got him now" and into the brush he jumped.

I grabbed the horn to keep from getting knocked off and to my amazement H Bomb bit that old cow in the butt and she let out a beller and took off out of there toward the herd. I kind of felt sorry for the cow I know how she felt since this physco horse had bit me in the butt before also. As soon as he bit her he turned around and jumped back out of the brush and I was still on board, things were looking up.

We made it to the foot of the mountains and camped for the night. Now I like camping but I am not a big fan of snakes, sneaky wiggling slimy, yea I said slimy, things. Yuck. So when you're sleeping under the stars that's the kind of stuff on your mind. One of sneaky things will join you in the sleeping bag. Yuck again. So I get laid out and trying not to think of the creepy crawly things in the night when

Max takes a rope and drags it across my sleeping bag.

"Agggggggggggg" I yelled as I jumped out of that mummy bag like I was greased. When I landed I was ten feet away picking up BIG rocks to attack with, when I looked over and saw Max and everybody else rolling around laughing at me. "Very funny" I said "you guys are so juvenile", a word I had read in a book and it seemed like a good time to use it.

I finally got to sleep, with one eye open, and before I knew it the sun was in my face and we were on the move again. We got saddled up, yep H Bomb again, and we went out and rounded up the ones that had wandered around and then we got started up the mountain.

We got started up the mountain and the trail we used was actually a very narrow canyon. It was only about three cows wide and in one spot they had to go single file and climb up over a three foot tall rock.

Nothing simple about moving the up the canyon other than they could not get back past us very easy.

We had to split up and we would each push a bunch of cows over the rock. When I got there H Bomb jumped up on the rock causing my saddle to slip back on his butt. The next jump then threw the saddle forward of course while this was going my head was snapping back and forth like the tip on a whip. But we finally landed on top and moved forward to where the valley opened up and we relaxed there for a while letting everybody rest up.

There were lots of nice Aspen trees in this area and of course we all have carved our names in them over the years and of course we had to again. So I headed over to do some carving leaving H Bomb staked out to eat. Not thinking he could do much just eating, after all he loved to eat.

I got back and was looking at my horse and something just didn't look right. I walked over to where he was and just stared at him and my saddle. My saddle was still on him where I left it, but it was covered, and I mean covered, in cow crap.

H Bomb had found the biggest, freshest cow pie he could and rolled in it. I know he did it deliberately, I know it. I mean that saddle and him were covered in steaming green/brown slimy cow poo. Dog food would be too good for him, I am thinking cat food would be better, or maybe just glue. Sell him to a glue factory and buy the first bottle that comes out and laugh every time I used it to glue something.

In the meantime I pulled a bunch of grass and wiped the saddle down as best I could. It was going to be sticky to sit in and made for a long day. I climbed on board and gingerly sat down. Yewww, it was wet and sticky, a very long day. Dead horse walking; I was planning his demise with every step.

After about an hour I forgot about the seat and was concentrating on moving cows. It was a long steep climb and they didn't want to move. We were working ourselves to death on them. Even H Bomb was getting irritated at them because he was biting them about every three steps. The poor dogs were all barked out and they were just biting when they could.

However they weren't always looking and one heeled H Bomb. He took to bucking and I mean he was getting it on. However because of the cow poo from earlier I was glued to the seat. I couldn't get off if I wanted, and I wanted. After a minute or so I got him stopped and I was still in the saddle. Everybody was yelling and clapping saying what a great ride.

I looked around to see who they were yelling for, they couldn't have been yelling at me, if I hadn't been glued to the saddle I would have fell off, but they were all looking at me. Max even said there was hope for me yet, yea right.

We finally arrived at the top and put them in a huge pasture where they would eat and grow fat for about a month when we would return and move them to another pasture. We headed for the summer camp where we would load up and haul the horses back down the mountain and home where they would have it easy for most of the summer now. But in the fall we would be at it again, rounding up the cows and moving them off the mountain. Same thing just in reverse this time. There would be other days with H Bomb for now he had a vacation coming and so did I.

## Haying with H-bomb

Well we had got the cows moved to the mountain for the summer. So the horses had the summer off to lie around and get fat except for a couple of trips to the mountain to move the cattle from one pasture to another. Since that only took a couple of times and was done in one day the horses got to lie around mostly. In fact I never took H-bomb on the first trip so he had it really easy getting fat and sassy, have to do something about that.

Since we had to irrigate to water the crops to grow stuff to feed the cattle all winter that meant we had to cut the hay and put it up also. Now this involved mowing the hay, raking the hay, baling the hay and then loading it, by hand, on a trailer and stacking it and then going to the hay corral and unloading it off the trailer and stacking it in a hay stack. Then of course you had to go to the hay stack in the winter time throw it off the hay stack on to the trailer and stack it on the trailer and then go out to the field it came off of and cut the strings and feed it to the cattle. So all in all that hay got man handled about six times before the cows ate it.

Now we had tractors and all the equipment we needed for this, and of course we had all the old equipment that was horse drawn from back in the day. The day was not that far gone from my day. I got to thinking about it and this sounded like something that H-bomb would be good for keeping him from lying around all summer and getting fat.

Now I didn't trust him with the mowing part but we had the old dump rake that was pulled by a horse and you sat on it and every so often would push on the trip leveler and dump out the hay, thus building a windrow from going round and round.

I got some grain out and shook it in a bucket in the horse pasture and here they came on the run, H-bomb leading the pack. The get to the corral and I shut the gate and give them all a little grain and when H-bomb finished his in about two bites I slipped a halter on him and let the rest out again. He looked at me like 'what's the big idea I'm on summer vacation' yea right I thought to myself.

I lead him over to the saddle shed and started hauling the harness out and putting it on H-bomb. He was looking at me like what the heck you doing, I told him that if I had to work all summer he had to work part of it and I figured that he could pull his load around here also.

So I explained to him as I lead him out of the corral over to the dump rake that he was going to pull the rake so we could put hay so he would have food to eat this winter. He looked at me like what the heck you talking about, more like he was thinking I am getting ready to make your day.

I got him all hooked up and crawled on board the rake and we headed out to the field and started making rounds. H-bomb was actually handling this fairly well he just plodded along and I was tripping the rake when it got full and after a couple of trips around the field we actually had a windrow developing.

The more rounds we made the more mundane it became and I was lost in thought, just running on autopilot tripping the dump; when it happened. All of a sudden H-bomb jumped sideways and took off at a run. I happened to see a snake crawling off when I went bouncing by but that was the last thing I got a good look at. We were going across the field headed for the barn and no matter what I did I could not get him to stop or slow up. All of a sudden I was in the air, we had hit a rock and I was bounced off the seat and fell in front of the rake.

I was being rolled along in the tines and hay like I was log. I was getting really dizzy and didn't know how much more I could take when we hit another rock and the rake tripped dumping the load and me with it. I lay there for what seemed like forever before the world finally stopped going around and around and around. I managed to get up without falling over and I was scratched up and looked like crap.

I looked around for H-bomb and seen him headed to the barn with the rake bouncing along behind him. I walked back to the house and mom seen me coming and asked why I was walking. I told her what had happed. We both looked at where H-bomb was standing by the corral and I looked at the rake. It was going to have to have some work done to it before it would be ready to go again so I walked over and got back on and parked the rake in line again and unhooked H-bomb and took him to the shed and got the harness off of him. I looked at him and said "you got lucky this time" and opened the gate to the horse pasture. He took a look at me and took off at high speed for about two hundred feet and then stopped and walked on.

I went back out and got my ford tractor fired up and hooked up to the side delivery rake and headed back out to the field. As I was driving away I looked at the horse pasture and there stood H-bomb looking at me and grinning, yes he was. You sorry SOB this was all a plan with you wasn't it?

That horse is getting smarter every day.

## The End

I have had H-bomb for years now; we got him when I was in JR high school and all though my high school years and a couple of years of college all of which came to an end this year. It was now the end of summer and I was getting ready to head off on my own see what was out there. I had managed to get a job working at the sale barn in Rapid City. My grandfather had worked there since before it was build, meaning he worked at the original sale barn, so I kind of had an in to the job.

H-bomb was no young colt when we bought him all those years ago at a horse sale in Billings; he already had quite a few years on him. Over the years that horse and I had been mortal enemies at least I thought so for a long time, I don't think he ever did. It seemed every time he bucked me off, left me a foot or dunked me in water he was always waiting for me or waiting for me at home, which is where he was always waiting, and he would nuzzle me and then turn and run off. Kind of like saying, "well, another day, I'll see you tomorrow" and away he would go.

As the years passed it became a job for me or maybe more of a contest to see who would win every time we would go riding and in those days it was all riding and it was all done on horseback. None of these 4-wheelers to run around on then, if you were lucky the best you would have would be an old broke down pickup or maybe even a go cart. But when it came to actually working cows, the horse was the only way back then.

We had lots of different horses to ride back then and they all got a work out, but like always we had favorites and we would use them as much as possible, the horses in my day were tough, they may have to work days on end, but when it was done they had it easy for weeks at a time with a little light riding once in awhile.

H-bomb was that to me, not exactly my favorite but not far from it, mainly because I couldn't let him win all the time, I had to show him who the boss was. We would go out and every ride was an adventure, some days he won and I would end up on the ground, some days he would leave me walking and some days he just bucked me off and waited for me to get back on as if to say "see, I can still do it."

Now as I stood there looking in the corral there he stood staring back at me trying to figure out what he could do to me next, I know that was what he was thinking. As I looked I could see the gray in his hair, he was getting old, I had no idea how old but he was getting up there, probable close to twenty if his teeth were anything to go by. It actually gave me an odd feeling to think of him as being old.

I walked into the corral and rubbed his neck and went to the saddle shed and got a bridle out, I put the saddle on and swung up and we took off. As I was riding along with him, his head down as low as it could get swinging back and forth pulling up a month full of grass every third or fourth swing, I thought back to all the times we had been out and he would do the same thing usually just before he bucked me off, thinking about it gave me a pause for a moment.

It was an easy ride. I remembered the time the chin strap broke and he ran off with me and I dropped a rope over that post in the middle of nowhere, I remembered that when I woke up and he woke up I had to ride him bare back to home, the thought brought a smile to me.

As we rode along we passed several ant hills and I remembered being bucked off into one and thought I had got away free and clear till about twenty minutes later a little red bugger was biting big chunks out of things best left unbitten and this all because of H-bomb.

As we were wandering around I looked at all the trees and brush on the river bottom and remembered the time that we were chasing a calf and I looked back at something and when I looked forward he had ran right under a tree branch that was about saddle high. I hit that thing and was knocked on my butt behind H-bomb. I had all the wind knocked out of me and I was wishing I was dead and when I could breathe again I thought that dirty rotten skunk had left me to walk. But no, he was standing there waiting for me to get up and back on. I couldn't believe it, but I never complained, the way I was feeling walking would have taken a week to get home.

There were more thoughts and adventures that I thought about on the ride, it was just a slow easy ride with my thoughts wandering. My last mistake with him because just as I was lost in thought he let out a big old fart and started bucking. I was all over that saddle pulling all the leather I could find but this time I stayed on board.  After a few minutes of this he stopped, looked back at me, wiggled an ear and we started off again.  Guess he decided it wasn't worth any more effort.

We got back to the house after a couple of hours of just wandering around.  I took him in the corral and tired him up by the saddle shed and got him unsaddled and brushed down.  I then got the hoof knife out and cleaned his hooves one last time. He never even laid on me as I did this.  It was at this point that I knew that he knew our time together was over.

I finished up rubbed his neck and behind his ears which I knew he liked and talked to him a few minutes telling him I was leaving to work someplace else with my grandfather but that I would be back once in a while to make sure he was behaving himself.  He just looked at me.  I walked over to the water tank and he followed me. I got to the tank and remembered the time I was shoeing him and he picked me up and dunked me in the tank.  H-bomb stuck his head in to take a drink so I stuck my hand in and splashed him, he jumped back and then walked up and stuck his head back in the water and shook it back and forth splashing me. I scratched him behind the ears again and walked out of the corral to the house. When I left the corral he was looking at me over the top rail. I turned and looked at him for minute and went to the house.

The next day I was leaving for my new job and I went out to the corral one last time to feed the livestock and when I got there H-bomb was there lying down. I whistled at him to get him up but he never moved. Not feeling good about this I crawled in to get him up but when I got there I could see he was gone. He was lying there with his eyes open but you could tell he was dead. I stood there looking down at that old brown nag with big tears falling off me, no matter how much I wiped them they just kept coming.

I finally went back to the house and told mom and dad about H-bomb and we all went back out and stood around looking at him. They brought up some of the stuff that he and I had been through and we talked and laughed told stories about him. But for me, I felt like something was gone.

Dad went and got the tractor with the backhoe on it and dug a grave down behind the buildings just a little way from the river. We then loaded him on a trailer and hauled him down and put him in the hole and I took over and did the job of burying him. It was the least I could do for him.

When I was done I sat there on the tractor just thinking. Mom and Dad went back to the house and left me with my thoughts.

"Goodbye my friend" I said and started the tractor and drove back to the house.